You Can't Catch Diabetes from a Friend

You Can't Catch

Diabetes from a Friend

By LYNNE KIPNIS and SUSAN ADLER

PHOTOGRAPHS by RICHARD BENKOF

 TRIAD SCIENTIFIC PUBLISHERS   GAINESVILLE, FLORIDA

AN ORIGINAL EDITORIAL DESIGN FROM
VISUAL BOOKS, Inc.
342 Madison Avenue, New York, N. Y. 10017

Library of Congress Cataloging in Publication Data

Kipnis, Lynne, 1955-
 You can't catch diabetes from a friend

 SUMMARY: Relates daily experiences of four children
who have diabetes.
 1. Diabetes in children — Juvenile literature.
 [1. Diabetes] I. Adler, Susan, 1954-   joint author.
II. Benkof, Richard. III. Title.
RJ420.D5K56   618.9'24'62   79-1165
ISBN 0-9600472-3-9

Published and Distributed by

Triad Publishing Company, Inc.
P.O. Box 13096
Gainesville, Florida 32604

PREFACE

Diabetes is a frightening subject. It is a disease that affects ten million people in the United States alone; one and one-half million have the juvenile-onset type, and over half of these are children. To dispel the fears and the multitude of misconceptions surrounding diabetes, all of which can be damaging to the diabetic, some education for the lay public is necessary.

While there are many books on this subject for adults, little of substance and clarity has been written for children. And there is a glaring need: the child who has diabetes must understand his disease if he is to take responsibility for its management; those around him must understand how diabetes affects his life if they are to treat him normally. This book was written for this young population — both diabetic and non-diabetic.

Although most physicians and health-care officials are in general agreement about the basic treatment of diabetes, considerable variation in the details does exist. It is not our purpose to debate the merits of these differences. The methods illustrated within reflect the pattern of therapy and advice of those professionals we consulted.

We are particularly grateful to members of the Division of Pediatric Metabolism at Washington University School of Medicine for their generous advice and support. To Karen, Danny, Colleen, and Robert, and their families, we give our deep thanks and admiration. And to our parents, the dedication of this book.

L.K. and S.A.
April 1979

This book is about Karen, Danny, Colleen, and

Some people think you can cure diabetes
by taking pills or other types of medicine.
   That's not true.
   Diabetes is an illness that never goes away.

Some people think you can get diabetes
from eating too much sugar.
   That's not true.
   Candy bars, cookies, soda pop, and other
sweets do not cause diabetes. But people who
have diabetes must limit the amount of sweet
foods they eat.

Robert – four children who have diabetes.

Diabetes doesn't show. People who have it are tall, short, fat, thin, adults, and children. You cannot tell if a person has diabetes just by looking at him or her.

Some people think you can get diabetes by being with somebody who has it.
That's not true.
You cannot catch diabetes from a friend.

This is Karen.

Karen is ten years old, and she has diabetes.

Most ten-year-olds have never heard of diabetes, and most people even older than that don't know very much about it. And no one knows what causes it, not even doctors.

But Karen has learned a great deal about diabetes. She knows that it is a disease that occurs when the body does not make enough of a chemical called *insulin*. This is something we all need to stay healthy. Karen knows that since her body doesn't make enough insulin, she has to make up for it by taking insulin injections.

Very early last Saturday morning her little brother, Michael, was dressed and ready to play.

"Karen," he called from her doorway. "Karen."

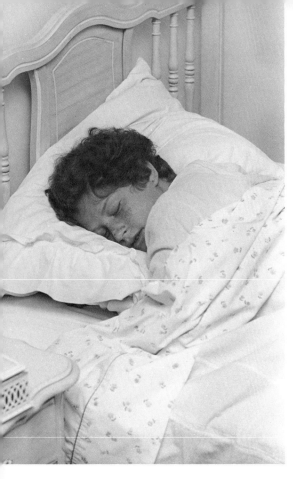

"Hey, Michael, I'm *sleeping*."
"But I want to play football," he shouted,
as he pounced on her bed.
"It's too early! Go away."

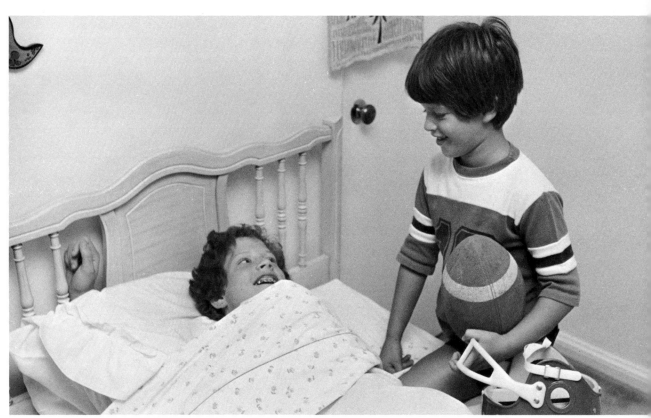

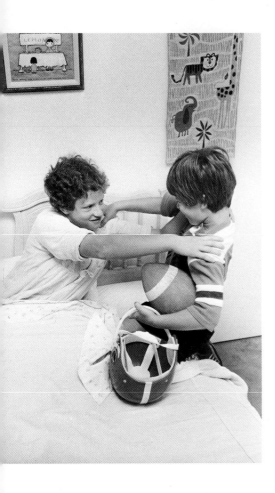

"But I'm already dressed!"

Michael was wearing his #12 sweatshirt and held his helmet. His football was tucked under his arm.

"C'mon, c'mon." Michael tugged at his sister.

Karen playfully tried to push him off the bed, but he wouldn't budge.

"Go find someone else to play with, Michael."

"I don't want to find someone else; I want to play with *you*."

"Later," she called from under the covers.

"Now."

"Later!"

"Now!"

Karen sat up in bed and looked straight at her brother. "I'm ... gonna ... get you!"

Michael tried to make a fast getaway — but it was too late. She pinned him down and began to tickle him.

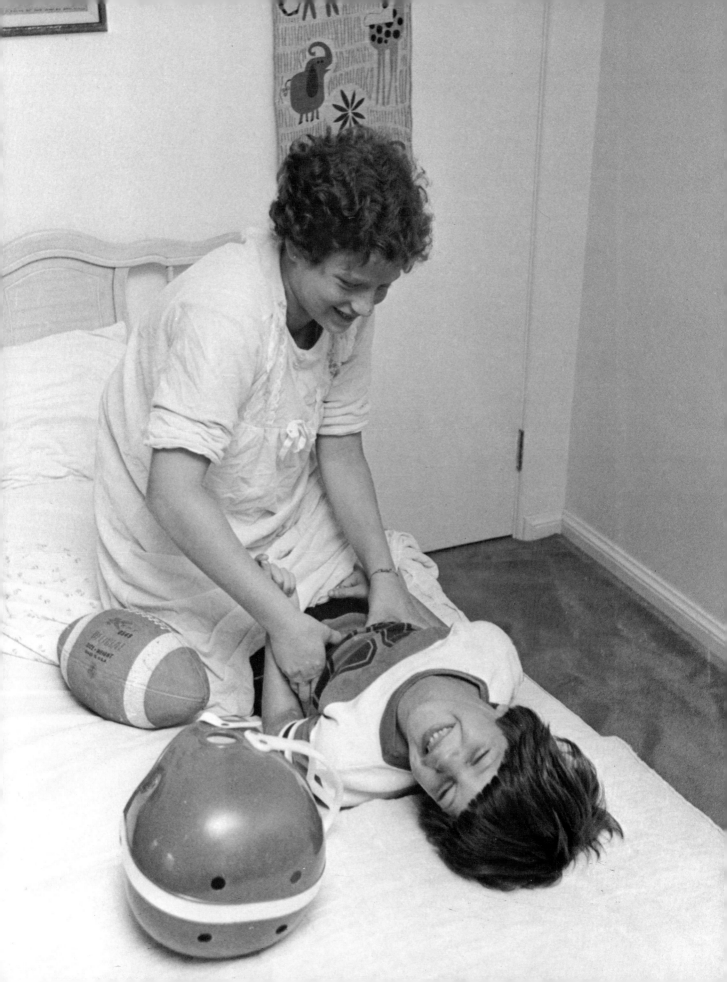

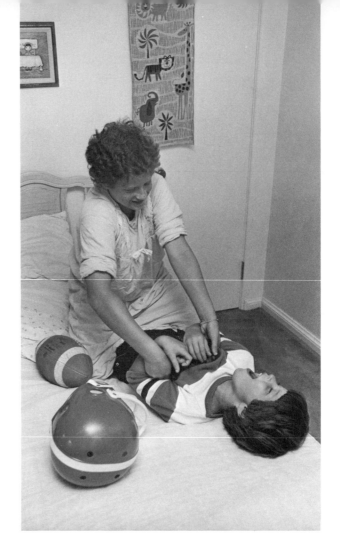

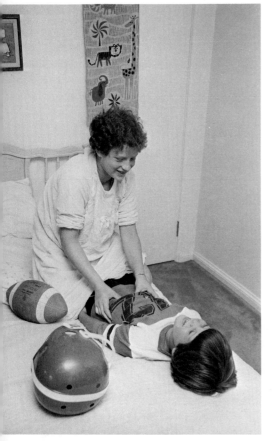

"Enough?" she asked.

He was laughing so hard he could barely say "No." She tickled him again.

"How about now?"

They were both laughing and Karen was wide awake.

"O.K.," she said, "we'll play football. Just give me some time to get dressed. Wait for me downstairs."

"Whoopee!" Michael shouted, and he raced out the door.

14

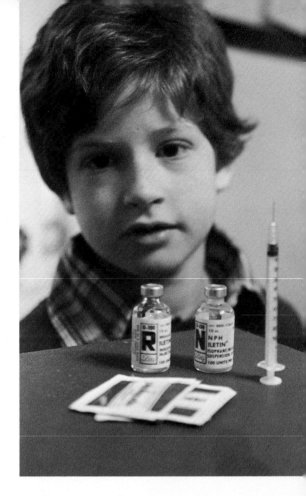

Karen knows that Michael hates to wait. When he wants Karen to hurry, he gets mad if she doesn't come right away. Still, Michael is learning that there are some things that come before playing football; for instance, both of them need to have breakfast. But even before that, Karen must start her day by giving herself an insulin injection.

When Karen first began taking insulin, both Michael and her sister Laura would watch. They were curious and interested and asked Karen a lot of questions.

"Why can't you take a pill or spoonful of medicine instead of a shot?"

"Because the insulin just won't work if I take it like aspirin or cough syrup."

"Let *me* give you the injection," Laura demanded.

"You don't know how to give injections," Karen said. "It's not an easy thing to do, unless someone has taught you how."

"Who taught you?" Michael asked somewhat enviously.

"The doctors and nurses at the hospital. They taught Mom and Dad, too."

"When will your diabetes go away?" asked Michael.

"It won't go away," Karen answered. "But the insulin will help keep me healthy."

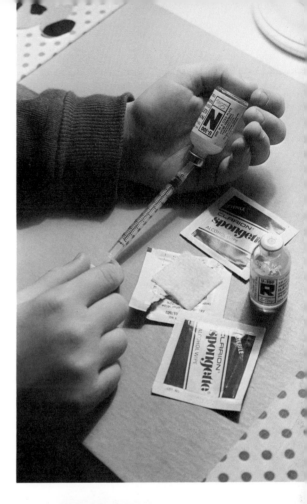

Michael and Laura have watched their sister give herself insulin injections many times.

First, Karen gets all the things she will need. She wipes the top of the insulin bottle with an alcohol swab so it will be clean. Next, she fills the syringe. Then she wipes her thigh with another alcohol swab and injects the insulin right in the middle of the spot she has cleaned.

And she's done!

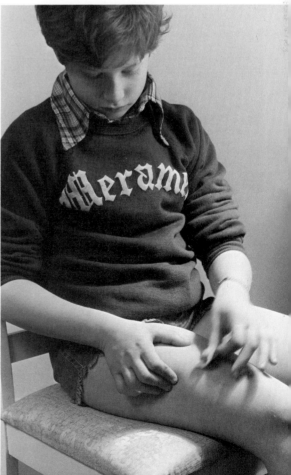

Karen gives herself two insulin injections every day — one before breakfast and the other before dinner. When she first started getting injections they hurt, and she was scared of them. She still doesn't *like* to get shots. Nobody does. But now she is so used to them that they hardly bother her at all.

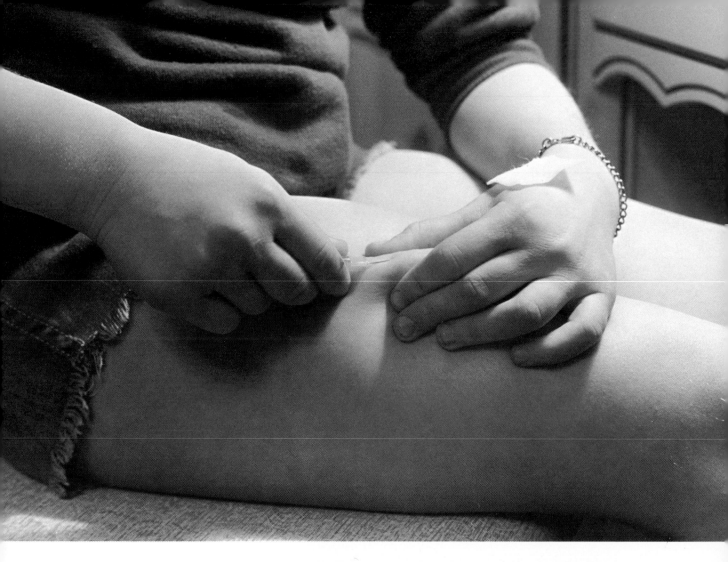

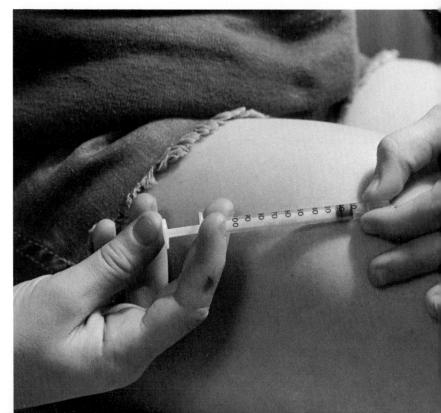

KAREN SCHNEIDER
Insulin Shot Rotation Chart

When most people need shots, they get them either in their arms or in their buttocks. But if Karen had insulin injections every day in the same arm, that arm would get very sore. So Karen and other kids with diabetes give themselves shots in their arms, their thighs, and even in their stomachs. Karen and her parents made up a chart to help her remember where she got her last shot and to show her where the next one should be.

This is Karen's family — her brother
Michael, her sister Laura, and her
mom and dad. Karen wasn't the only
person to make a lot of changes
because of her diabetes. Her whole
family felt the effects of the disease;
everyone was changed a bit.

"Ever since we found out about
Karen's disease," Laura complained,
"my parents have given her so much
attention — sometimes I think more

to her than to me or Michael. I guess
they don't do it on purpose — it just
happens. Still, it seems like Karen
never has to feed the dog, she *always*
gets to sit up front in the car, and she
can *always* have friends come over to
our house.

"I remember a couple of months ago I wanted to go to the
movies with one of my friends. My parents wouldn't let me.
They said that we weren't old enough to go alone.

"I got really angry at them. I yelled, 'I bet if I had diabetes
you'd let me do what I want. You're always letting Karen do
what she wants. She's your favorite.'

"Those were mean things for me to say. I didn't *really* wish

I had diabetes — and I know my parents don't have favorites.
But sometimes it still feels like Karen always gets her way."

THIS IS DANNY.

Danny is eleven years old and has diabetes like Karen. And, like Karen, he gives himself insulin injections every morning and every evening.

On weekdays Danny walks to school with his friends. After a morning of reading and studying, his class spends the last half hour before lunch working independently in their math workbooks. It's hard to do math problems when your stomach is growling! But finally the bell rings, and everyone races down the hall to the cafeteria.

As usual, Danny eats with Ross and Darren and Jeff, his best friends.

"I'm starving!" said Ross. "Ick — I've got egg salad today."

"You think that's bad," moaned Jeff, "I've got meatloaf again. I *hate* meatloaf!"

"I know what kind of sandwich I have without even looking — peanut butter and jelly." Darren opened his lunch bag. "See? I was right. Danny, what do you have?"

"Salami."

"Wow! I like salami sandwiches," said Darren. "Let's trade. Hey, I've got a great idea; why don't we all trade?"

"Good idea," said Ross.

"Yeah," said Jeff.

"Sorry guys," Danny said. "I can't trade."

"How come?" they asked him.

"Well, you know that you couldn't eat ten ice cream sandwiches for lunch and a whole package of hot dogs for dinner, with junk food in between, and still stay healthy...."

They all nodded.

"And everybody needs vitamins and proteins and sugars and starches and fats."

Ross laughed. "You sound just like my mom. But you still didn't tell us why you can't trade sandwiches."

"I have diabetes, you know, so my body has some trouble using sugars and starches — foods like bread, potatoes, cake, and ice cream."

"You mean you can't *ever* have milk shakes or mashed potatoes — what about candy?" Ross asked. "Did you get diabetes from eating too much candy?"

"No, I didn't say that — you don't *get* diabetes from eating candy or stuff like that," Danny answered. "But since I have diabetes, I just have to eat less of some things. The reason I can't trade sandwiches is that I have to stick to the meal plan my parents and I make every morning."

Jeff was impressed. "That must be a lot of work."

"Oh, no; it's easy," Danny said. "Our family had really good lessons from the doctors and nurses at

the hospital. They even taught us how to measure what I eat; sometimes we weigh foods that are hard to measure.

"When I follow my meal plan, the food I eat works together with the insulin I take to keep me healthy."

After school, Danny went over to Darren's house. Darren's mom greeted them at the door.

"Hi, boys," she said, as they put their books on the kitchen counter.

Darren opened the refrigerator door, looking around for something to eat.

"If you're hungry there are cookies in the cookie jar," she told them. "Help yourself, Danny."

"Could I have an apple instead?" Danny asked.

"Are you sure you don't want a cookie?"

"I'd rather have an apple because I had cookies at lunch."

"It has to do with his diabetes, Mom," Darren said. "He explained it to us today at school."

"I told them that I couldn't trade what was in my lunchbox —" Danny began.

"— but he was really explaining diabetes, Mom."

"I see," said Darren's mom, handing Danny an apple.

Now, whenever Danny says that he can't trade his salami sandwich for a peanut butter and jelly sandwich or his popsicle for a banana, his friends understand. They know that Danny has to be just a little more careful about what he eats than they do.

This is Danny's family — his brothers Kenny and Mike, and his mom and dad. Danny's family also felt the effects of the disease; everyone was changed a bit.

"I think my parents watch Danny too closely," said Mike. "They're always asking him if he feels O.K. or if he took his insulin shot. They're always telling him what to do, telling him things he already knows.

"Like last Halloween, when we all went trick-or-treating. We dressed up as gangsters and took large sacks to collect candy in.

"Danny *knew* he couldn't eat his Halloween candy. But while we were getting dressed my mom and dad said to him, 'Remember, Danny, don't eat any of the candy you collect.' And they didn't tell him just once, they told him three or four times.

"I don't know why they do that; Danny knows what he can eat and what he can't. He could recite everything about diabetes backwards if you asked him to.

"We got so much candy that night! I ate lots of mine right away; Kenny saved his and wouldn't let anyone have even one piece; but we didn't know what to do with all the stuff Danny collected.

"Then Dad had a great idea — he decided to pay Danny a penny for each piece of candy in his bag. Wow! Danny made over two dollars that night!"

THIS IS COLLEEN.

She is seven years old and has diabetes just like Karen and Danny. She also takes insulin injections daily and has her own special meal plan.

Because she has diabetes, it is important for her to see her doctor for regular check-ups. At each visit Colleen undresses, and Dr. Weldon checks her heart, her ears, her nose and throat, and her urine.

All last week Colleen felt fine, but she still had to see Dr. Weldon two times. On Monday she went in for her regular check-up, but the doctor found something wrong: Colleen had sugar in her urine. Most people don't have sugar in their urine.

The sugar that Dr. Weldon found is not the kind you sprinkle on your cereal, but a type of sugar called *glucose*. Colleen knows that most of the time the insulin she takes and the food she eats work together to keep her healthy. Glucose in her urine is a sign that her body is having trouble using sugars and starches. The more glucose there is, the more trouble Colleen's body is having.

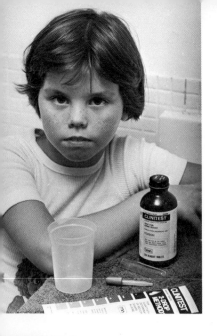

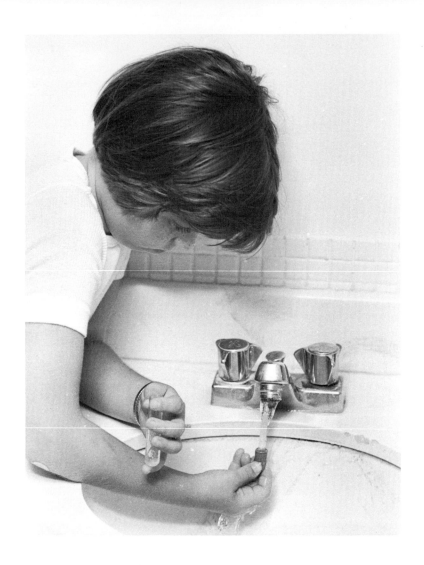

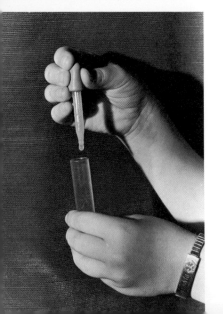

Three times every day, Colleen tests her urine for glucose: before breakfast, before lunch, and before bedtime. She uses a kit the doctor gave her that contains a plastic cup, a test tube, a dropper, some tablets, and a color chart. The test takes only a minute. She first urinates into the plastic cup. Then, with the dropper she puts two drops of her urine into the test tube and adds ten drops of water from the faucet; then she drops one tablet into the test tube. For 15-20 seconds the tablet makes the mixture bubble.

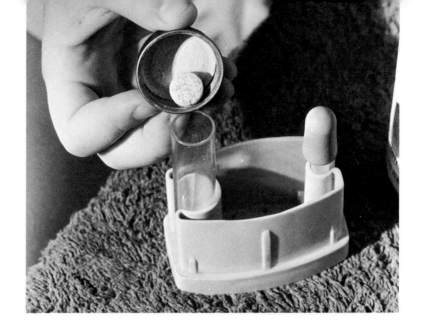

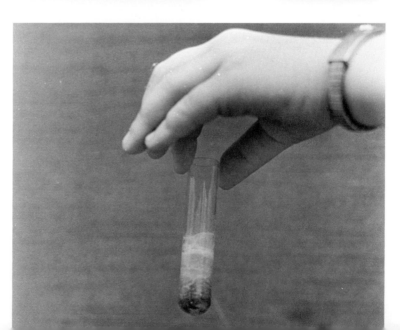

When the bubbling stops, the urine and water have turned a different color. A blue color means that there is no glucose in her urine. Green means there is some glucose, but only a little. But when the mixture in the test tube turns orange, Colleen and her parents know there is a lot of glucose in her urine, and if that happens too often they must call the doctor. Colleen knows that the tests are important, so she keeps a notebook where she writes down the colors of all the tests.

At the same time that Colleen is testing her urine for glucose, she also tests it for *ketones*. Ketones occur when the body is not using fats and proteins properly. Colleen uses the dropper to place one drop of urine on another kind of tablet, then waits a moment to see if it changes color. If it does not change, that means there are no ketones. If it becomes slightly darker, there are some ketones. But if it becomes a really dark purple, it is a warning that Colleen's body is having trouble, and she needs to tell her doctor.

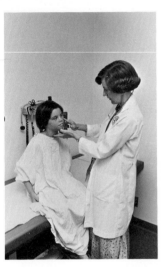

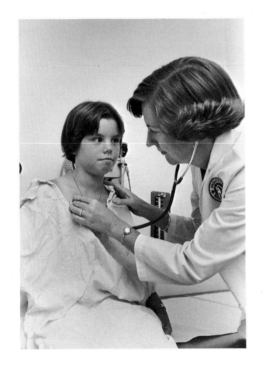

That Monday at her check up, Colleen
sat on the examining table and watched

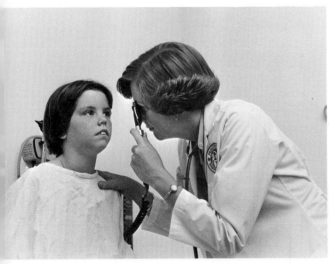

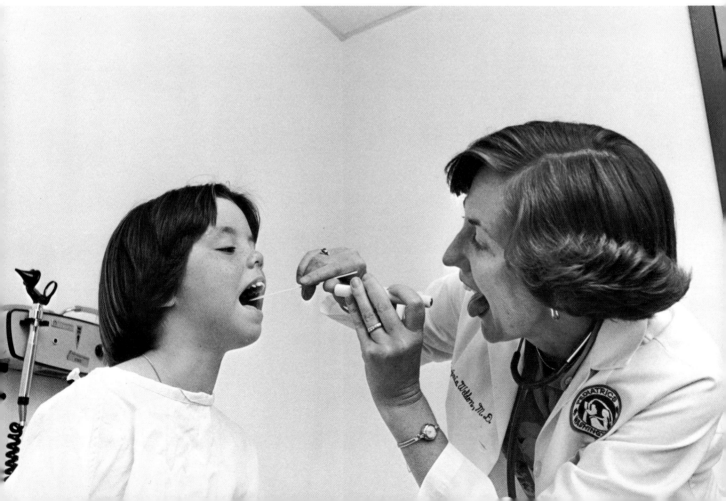

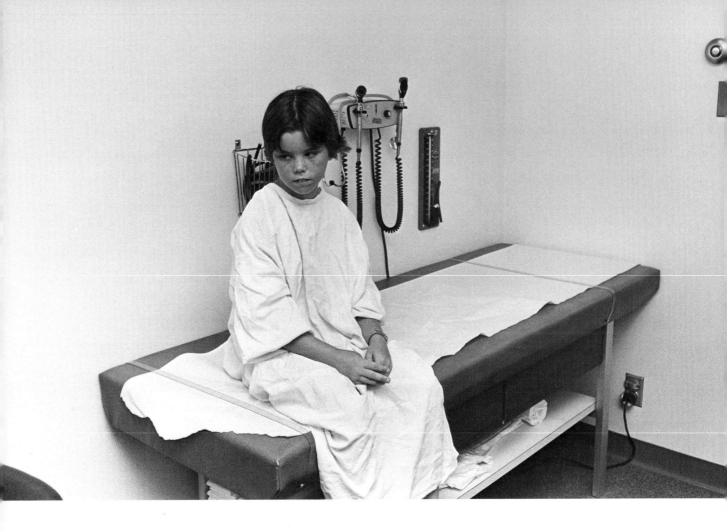

as Dr. Weldon looked through the notebook. Colleen's urine had just tested orange, showing a lot of glucose. But the notebook had no orange tests written in it at all — only blue and green.

"I don't understand," the doctor told Colleen, "why I find so much glucose in your urine and you find so little. Are you sure that you are using the kit the way we taught you? Are you writing down the right color for each test? I hope you are following your meal plan and taking the right amount of insulin. Are you taking your injections at the same time every day? Are you eating sweets?"

Colleen looked very uncomfortable. She was scared of all the questions. She was scared when the urine test turned orange. She was scared when Dr. Weldon looked at her notebook. She hadn't wanted to come in for the check-up. She wanted to go home.

Colleen started to cry. The doctor sat down on the table beside her.

"Let's talk about what's upsetting you, O.K.?"

Colleen just shrugged her shoulders.

"Can't you tell me what's wrong?"

Colleen sat very still. Finally, she told Dr. Weldon the truth.

"I really have been following my meal plan and taking my insulin and testing my urine. Most of the urine tests really were blue or green, just like I wrote in my notebook."

Colleen paused.

"Were there orange tests, too?" asked the doctor.

Colleen nodded. "Sometimes. Then I got scared. My parents would think I was doing something wrong if they saw 'orange' in my notebook, and they would be worried. So I just wrote down 'blue' or 'green' every time, even when the test turned out orange."

The doctor hugged her and told her she understood.

"I know that it's scary to be doing every-thing right and still see the orange color

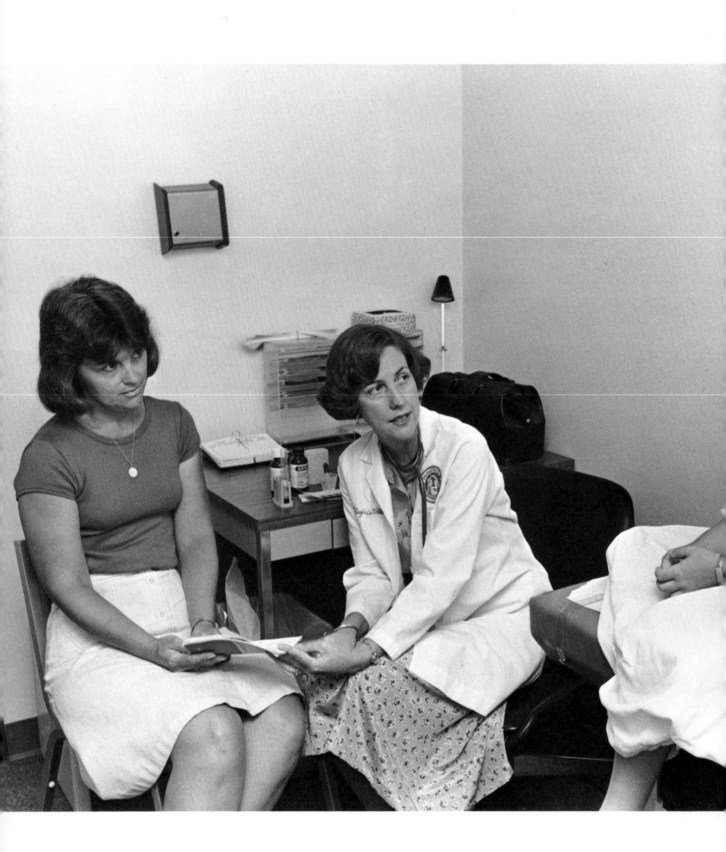

in your tests," she said. "But it is very important to tell your parents and me whenever that happens. That way you'll be helping all of us, and I can try to figure out what is wrong. Most of the time, following the meal plan and taking your insulin will keep you healthy; you can tell how well the food and insulin are working by the amount of glucose in your urine. But other times you'll be doing everything right and you'll feel fine, like now, and there will *still* be a lot of glucose in your urine. That's not your fault. Sometimes your body has more trouble with diabetes than at other times.

Colleen felt much better. After she dressed, the doctor talked to her and her mother.

"Colleen, I want you to take more insulin in the morning injection — I'll write down the amount for you. Maybe that will better control the amount of sugar your body uses and reduce the glucose in your urine. Our next visit on Friday should tell."

This is Colleen's family — her sisters Kathleen and Maureen, her brother Dan, and her mom and dad. Colleen's whole family felt the effects of the disease; everyone was changed a bit.

"Colleen never liked to talk about her diabetes," said her mom. "I think it embarrassed her.

"Her father and I had a hard time explaining the disease to her brother and sisters. We didn't know how much to tell them, because we didn't know how much they'd understand.

"Imagine how worried they were about Colleen, seeing their sister taking injections and testing her urine. And I know that they sensed our concern. It would have been better not to keep things from them, but we didn't realize that at the time.

"Then one day something very nice happened. The kids were all downstairs in the basement. They were so quiet, I walked by the door to make sure they were O.K. What I heard was Colleen talking — explaining to them for the first time — about her diabetes. Well, I'm not sure why she told them, but I do know the kids felt a lot less worried after that. That talk was a big step forward — for everyone."

THIS IS ROBERT.

He is fourteen years old and
has diabetes. Like Karen and
Danny and Colleen, Robert
takes insulin injections, follows
a meal plan, tests his urine, and
has regular check-ups.

During the summer, Robert
and his friend James earn
spending money by cutting
lawns in their neighborhood.
James spends his money on
comic books — he has stacks of
them in his bedroom. Robert
uses his money to buy models
— models of cars, vans, planes,
and boats.

Sometimes his friends tease
him about all his models. "You
already have a million vans.
Get an airplane."

"But I like vans," Robert tells them every time. "They're
more fun to put together."

To Robert, models are like puzzles. The harder they are to
build, the better he likes them. He paints and decorates each
one and puts it on a shelf in his room. For Christmas, his aunt
and uncle gave him a huge model of a battleship. It had more
pieces than any model Robert had ever seen before. At first it
was confusing because he wasn't sure where all the pieces
went. But once he fit the larger parts together, he could figure
out the rest.

To build models, all Robert has to know are the basics. And
the basics are all Robert's friends need to know about his
diabetes.

"Hey, Robert!" his friend Tom yelled from the front yard, "What are you doing today?"

"I'm cutting lawns with James. What are *you* going to do?"

"Nothing. Look, Robert, I've got a pair of clippers; how about if I help you and James cut grass?"

"Well," Robert said. "it's O.K. with me, but I've got to check with James first. We're partners, you know."

"I'll go and get my clippers."

"O.K. Meet us back here as soon as you can."

A few minutes later James crossed Robert's front yard, pulling his lawnmower behind him. "Ready to start?" he called.

"Tom's helping today. He'll be right back, O.K.?"

"Sure."

They both sat down on Robert's porch and waited. Pretty soon Tom came running up to the gate. "Let's go!" he hollered.

Robert and James picked up their equipment, and the three of them took off down the street.

Mrs. Parker lived the closest, so they cut her lawn first — James mowing, Tom trimming, and Robert sweeping. They worked fast because they wanted to have all their jobs finished by lunchtime when the sun was hottest.

Robert was almost done sweeping the cut grass off the pavement when he suddenly started to sweat and his heart beat very fast. He felt so dizzy that he was afraid he would fall over, so he quickly sat down on the step.

James noticed Robert first; he dropped his mower and raced over to see what was wrong.

"Do you have any sugar with you?" James asked anxiously. Robert was already searching his pockets. "Here, let me help you." James found the package of sugar and opened it for Robert. Robert swallowed the sugar.

"Hey, guys —" Tom had noticed his friends sitting down. "What's wrong? Are you sick, Robert?" Tom came and sat by Robert and James.

"He's having an insulin reaction," James told him. "He'll be O.K. in a couple of minutes because he just ate some sugar."

"An insulin reaction? What's that?" Tom asked.

"You know Robert has diabetes, don't you?"

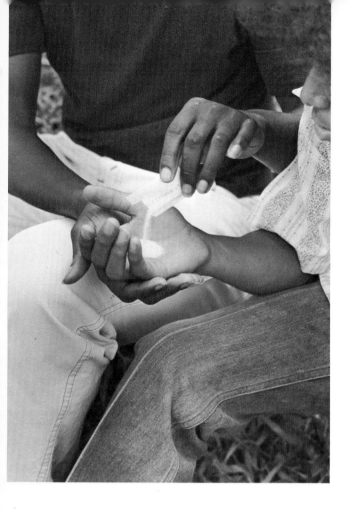

"Sure."

"Well, sometimes when he works too hard," James explained, "his body starts running out of sugar and he gets dizzy and sweats a lot and feels really sick. That's why he stopped sweeping and sat down. You feel better yet, Robert?"

"Yeah, much better," Robert answered. He turned to Tom. "If you ever see me having an insulin reaction, just make sure I eat some sugar. I always keep a package of sugar in my pocket, but candy or soda pop would work just as well. Usually I feel better after that."

"But if not," James added, "we help him home so that his aunt can call his doctor right away."

"What happens if you get sick and no one knows you're having an insulin reaction?" Tom asked Robert.

"That's how come I wear this medallion. You see right here?" Robert held up the chain. "It says I'm diabetic."

For fifteen minutes the boys sat on the step to rest.

"Hey," Tom said, all of a sudden, "I won't catch your diabetes, will I?"

"Don't worry," Robert told him. "You can't get diabetes from me; it's not a disease you can catch from someone."

It was nearly noon when they finished all the lawns. Finally, they had earned enough money to buy what they wanted.

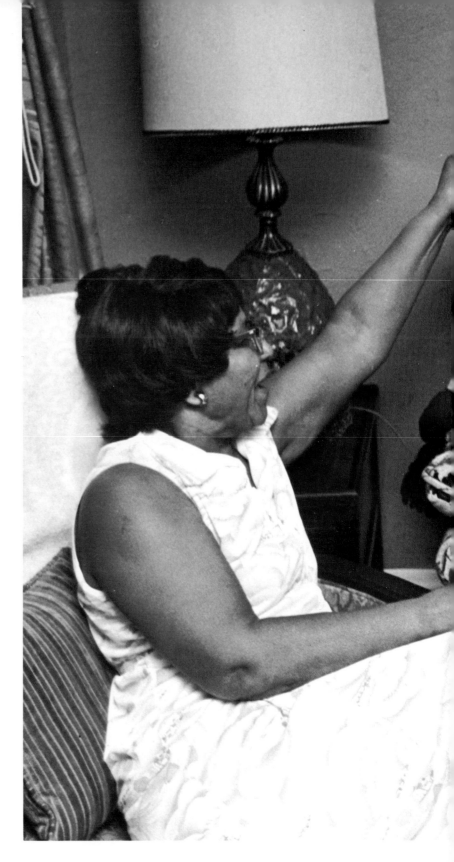

"Back already, Robert?" his
aunt asked, as he ran in the
front door. She was sitting with
his uncle in the living room.

"Yeah, there were three of us
today. Tom helped out."

"How about some lunch?"

"I've got to get something.
I'll be back in a few minutes."

"No. Eat your sandwich first.
You don't want to get sick, do
you?"

"I'll eat it on the way."

Robert grabbed the sandwich,
stuffed a bite in his mouth, and
raced out the door. He had his
money in his pocket.

"Well, his uncle said, smiling,
turning to his aunt, "we know
what that boy's off to buy!"

This is Robert's family — his aunt and uncle. He has lived with them ever since he was two years old. They also felt the effects of Robert's disease; they both were changed a bit.

"Before we found out about Robert's diabetes," his uncle said, "our household was a lot more flexible. If I was late coming home from work, we would just eat later. But now, Robert and his aunt start dinner without me."

"We're on a tighter schedule," added his aunt. Insulin shots and urine tests are done at certain times each day, and meals must be eaten at certain times, too.

"Robert always has to have meals at regular times after his insulin injection. When he gets more exercise than usual, it's a good idea for him to have a snack first. If the amount of insulin and the amount of food get out of balance, he could have an insulin reaction."

"We like to go out for dinner on Wednesdays," said his uncle. "That's our special family night. We go to different restaurants, but I have a favorite one where all the waitresses know me. Robert kids me because I always order the same thing — baked chicken and dumplings.

"That's where we went last Wednesday. Usually it's not very crowded and we get seated quickly. But last week the hostess told us we'd have to wait an hour. No way! We just couldn't wait that long; Robert had to eat. So we went off to another restaurant where we could get served right away.

"We've learned to expect some problems, like what happened last Wednesday. This week, though, we're going to try that restaurant again. Robert is already kidding me about my chicken and dumplings!"

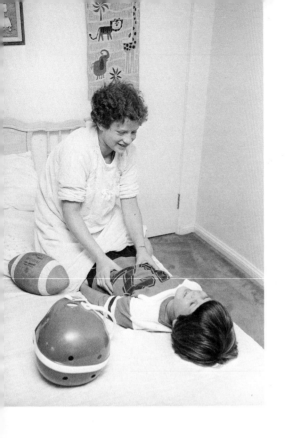

Karen, Danny, Colleen, and Robert are four of almost one million young people in the United States who have diabetes. All of them need to take insulin, plan their meals, and test their urine every day. They also need to have regular check-ups. Then, they can all lead active, normal lives.